bitesize

TARTLETS, QUICHETTES
& CUTE THINGS

hardie grant books
MELBOURNE · LONDON

contents

chicken meatballs
wrapped in prosciutto

Preheat the oven to 180°C (350°F/Gas 4). Line 2 baking trays with baking paper.

Place the chicken, haloumi, lemon zest, parsley, egg yolk and breadcrumbs in a bowl, season with salt and pepper and combine well. Shape into golf-ball-sized rounds.

Cut the prosciutto into thick strips, wide enough to wrap around the meatballs. Wrap each ball with a strip of prosciutto and place on the tray. Bake for 10–12 minutes or until cooked through.

MAKES 24

500 g (1 lb 2 oz) minced chicken

100 g (3½ oz/1 cup) grated haloumi cheese

finely grated zest of 1 lemon

2 tablespoons chopped flat-leaf (Italian) parsley or sage

1 egg yolk

50 g (1¾ oz/½ cup) dried breadcrumbs

sea salt and freshly ground black pepper

10–12 slices prosciutto

prawn and chorizo
pinchos with paprika mayonnaise

Preheat the oven to 180°C (350°F/Gas 4).

Place the cherry tomatoes on a baking tray, drizzle with the oil and season with salt. Roast for 10–12 minutes or until just beginning to collapse.

Meanwhile, brush one side of the baguette slices with the oil, place on a baking tray and bake for 8–10 minutes or until toasted and crisp.

To make the mayonnaise, combine the ingredients in a small bowl and refrigerate until required.

Preheat a barbecue or char-grill pan to high. Cook the chorizo until crisp on both sides. Drain on kitchen paper.

To serve, spread the baguette slices with the mayonnaise, top with a slice of chorizo, half a prawn, a cherry tomato and garnish with the parsley. Skewer with a toothpick to serve if desired.

MAKES 24

250 g (9 oz/1 punnet) small cherry tomatoes, large ones halved

olive oil, for drizzling

sea salt

1 small baguette, cut into 24 thin slices

1 chorizo sausage, cut into 24 thin slices

12 cooked prawns (shrimp), peeled, deveined and halved lengthways

⅓ cup flat-leaf (Italian) parsley leaves

PAPRIKA MAYONNAISE

250 g (9 oz/1 cup) good-quality mayonnaise

1 teaspoon smoked sweet paprika

1 tablespoon lime juice

brioche with scrambled eggs
and salmon caviar

To make the dough, combine the yeast, sugar and 2 tablespoons warm water in a small bowl and leave in a warm place for 5–10 minutes or until frothy.

Place the flour and salt in the bowl of an electric mixer fitted with a dough hook and make a well in the centre. Add the yeast mixture, egg and butter and mix on low speed to combine. Knead for 6–8 minutes or until smooth and no longer sticky. Transfer to a floured bowl, cover with a kitchen towel and leave in a warm place for 1–2 hours or until doubled in size.

Preheat the oven to 190°C (375°F/Gas 5). Line 2 baking trays with baking paper. Knock back the dough and knead on a floured surface for 1–2 minutes. Roll pieces of dough into 2 cm (¾ inch) balls and place on the trays. Flatten each slightly, cover with a kitchen towel and leave in a warm place for 20 minutes or until doubled in size. Bake for 10–15 minutes or until golden and the bottoms sound hollow when tapped.

To serve, whisk the eggs and cream together and season with salt and pepper. Heat a heavy-based frying pan over medium heat. Add the butter and egg mixture and cook, stirring frequently, for 3–4 minutes or until just set. Remove the pan from the heat; the residual heat in the pan will set the eggs.

To serve, halve each brioche, fill with a spoonful of the scrambled eggs and 4–5 pearls of salmon caviar, and garnish with the chives.

MAKES 25–30

3 eggs

2 tablespoons pouring (single) cream

sea salt and freshly ground black pepper

40 g (1½ oz) butter

50 g (1¾ oz) salmon caviar (roe)

snipped chives, for garnish

BRIOCHE DOUGH

2 x 7 g (½ oz) sachets dried yeast

1 teaspoon caster sugar

200 g (7 oz/1⅓ cup) plain (all-purpose) flour, sifted

1 teaspoon salt

2 eggs, lightly beaten

60 g (2¼ oz) unsalted butter, melted

peking duck pancakes

To make the batter, lightly whisk the egg, milk and salt together in a bowl. Whisk in the flour, a little at a time, until the batter is the consistency of thin custard. Leave to rest for 30 minutes. Strain the batter, if there are any lumps. Stir through the chives.

Heat a small, heavy-based frying pan over medium heat. Brush the pan with the butter and pour in just enough batter to form a 10 cm (4 inch) pancake. Cook for 1–2 minutes or until golden, then flip over and cook the other side until golden. Remove from the pan and repeat with the remaining batter.

Preheat the oven to 180°C (350°F/Gas 4). Place the duck on a baking tray and bake for 8–10 minutes or until just heated through. Remove and thinly slice.

To serve, gently warm the pancakes in the oven. Lay the pancakes on a surface and spread with a little hoisin sauce. Place 1–2 slices of duck, some lettuce, cucumber and coriander leaves in the centre of each pancake and roll up. Serve with extra hoisin sauce for dipping.

MAKES ABOUT 20

200 g (7 oz) pre-cooked duck breast, skin discarded

hoisin sauce, for spreading and dipping

¼ iceberg lettuce, shredded

1 Lebanese (short) cucumber, cut into long, thin strips

1 cup coriander (cilantro) leaves

PANCAKES

1 egg

250 ml (9 fl oz/1 cup) milk

pinch of salt

150 g (5½ oz/1 cup) plain (all-purpose) flour

1 tablespoon snipped chives

30 g (1 oz) butter, melted

salmon and mango
ceviche in endive boats

Cut the salmon into 5 mm (¼ inch) dice and place in a non-reactive bowl. Add the lime juice, zest, chilli and onion and stir well. Cover and refrigerate for 20–30 minutes.

Add the mango and coriander to the ceviche and stir well.

Trim the bases of the endive, separate the leaves and arrange on a serving platter. Spoon the ceviche into the leaves and drizzle with the oil. Serve with the lime wedges.

MAKES ABOUT 24

250 g (9 oz) piece of skinless
  salmon fillet, pin-boned

3 tablespoons lime juice

½ teaspoon finely grated
  lime zest

½ long green chilli, finely diced

½ small red onion, finely diced

1 mango, diced

2 tablespoons chopped
  coriander (cilantro)

2 heads Belgian endive

extra-virgin olive oil,
  for drizzling

lime wedges, to serve

preserved lemon, chicken
and radicchio quichettes

To make the pastry, place the flour, butter and salt in a food processor and pulse until the mixture resembles breadcrumbs. Add the egg yolk and 2 tablespoons cold water and pulse again until just starting to come together. Knead on a floured surface to bring together, shape into a disc, wrap in plastic wrap and refrigerate for 1 hour.

Preheat the oven to 180°C (350°F/Gas 4). Lightly grease twenty-four 6 cm x 2 cm (2½ inch x ¾ inch) fluted or plain tartlet tins. Roll out the pastry to 5 mm (¼ inch) thick and, using an 8 cm (3¼ inch) round cutter, cut out 24 circles. Press each circle into the tins, trimming excess pastry. Place on baking trays and refrigerate for 30 minutes. To blind bake the cases, line them with baking paper and fill with dried beans, rice or baking weights. Bake for 15–20 minutes, remove the beans and paper and bake for a further 10–15 minutes or until golden and cooked through. Remove and set aside to cool in the tins.

Meanwhile, heat the oil in a frying pan over medium–high heat. Add the chicken and cook for 1–2 minutes. Add the radicchio and preserved lemon and cook for 2 minutes or until the chicken is cooked through and the radicchio is wilted. Season with pepper.

Divide the mixture between the cases. Whisk together the eggs and cream in a jug and pour into the cases. Bake for 15–20 minutes or until golden and set. Cool slightly and remove from tins.

To serve, top each quichette with a tomato quarter and garnish with the herbs.

MAKES 24

1 tablespoon olive oil

140 g (5 oz) skinless chicken breast fillet, finely diced

70 g (2⅔ oz/2 cups) finely chopped radicchio

¼ preserved lemon, flesh discarded and rind finely diced

freshly ground black pepper

2 large eggs

3 tablespoons pouring (single) cream

6 cherry tomatoes, quartered

fresh micro herbs, for garnish

SHORTCRUST PASTRY

300 g (10½ oz/2 cups) plain (all-purpose) flour

180 g (6⅓ oz) cold unsalted butter, cubed

pinch of salt

1 egg yolk

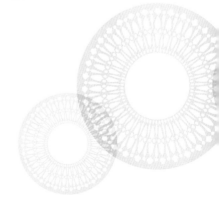

brioche with orange,
fennel and grapes

Combine the milk, sugar and yeast in a small bowl, set aside in a warm place for 5–10 minutes or until frothy and the sugar has dissolved.

Place the flour, ground fennel and orange zest in the bowl of an electric mixer fitted with a dough hook and make a well in the centre. Add the egg and the yeast mixture and mix on low speed to combine. While mixing, add the butter, in batches, until well incorporated and continue mixing for 10–15 minutes or until the dough is soft, glossy and comes away from the side of the bowl. Transfer to a floured bowl, cover with a kitchen towel and leave in a warm place for 1½ hours or until doubled in size.

Preheat the oven to 180°C (350°F/Gas 4). Lightly grease twenty-four 6 cm x 2 cm (2½ inch x ¾ inch) fluted brioche moulds. Knock back the dough and divide into 24 pieces. Shape each into a ball and place in the moulds. Cover with a kitchen towel and leave in a warm place for 30 minutes or until doubled in size. Brush the tops with the egg yolk and bake for 25 minutes or until golden and the bottoms sound hollow when tapped. Turn out from the moulds and cool on a wire rack.

To serve, make a 3 cm (1¼ inch) long incision along the top of the brioche on an angle to reach halfway down and fill the pocket with the goat's cheese and grape halves.

MAKES 24

3 tablespoons milk

2 tablespoons caster (superfine) sugar

1 x 7 g (¼ oz) sachet dried yeast

300 g (10½ oz/2 cups) plain (all-purpose) flour, sifted, plus extra, for dusting

1 tablespoon fennel seeds, toasted and ground

finely grated zest of 1 orange

3 eggs, lightly beaten

120 g (4¼ oz) unsalted butter, cubed and at room temperature

2 egg yolks, lightly beaten

250 g (9 oz) goat's cheese

24 grapes, halved lengthways

crisp mushrooms
stuffed with goat's cheese

Combine the goat's cheese, garlic, herbs and cream in a bowl and season with pepper. Remove the stems from the mushrooms. Use a teaspoon to spoon the mixture into the mushroom cavities, rounding the tops to form 'balls'.

Lightly whisk the egg and milk together in a bowl. Place the flour and breadcrumbs in separate shallow dishes. Working with one mushroom at a time, coat each one in flour, then dip in the eggwash and coat in the breadcrumbs. Repeat so that the mushrooms are double coated to prevent any leakage during cooking.

Heat the oil in a deep-fryer or large, heavy-based saucepan to 180°C (350°F) and deep-fry 6–8 mushrooms at a time for 3–4 minutes or until golden. Drain on kitchen paper.

MAKES 24

150 g (5½ oz) goat's cheese or ricotta

2 garlic cloves, crushed

2 tablespoons chopped mixed herbs, such as basil, parsley, thyme or oregano

1 tablespoon thickened cream

freshly ground black pepper

24 button mushrooms

1 egg

125 ml (4½ fl oz/½ cup) milk

plain (all-purpose) flour, for coating

50–100 g (1¾–3½ oz/½–1 cup) dried breadcrumbs

vegetable oil, for deep-frying

grilled eggplant
and chickpea fritters

Cut the eggplant into 1 cm (½ inch) thick slices and place on a tray. Sprinkle with salt and leave for 20 minutes or until beads of liquid form on the surface. Rinse the eggplant and dry well. Brush with a little oil and cook under a hot grill (broiler) until tender and browned on each side. Leave to cool, then roughly chop.

Place the flour in a large bowl and season with salt and pepper. Add the milk and eggs and beat until combined and smooth. Stir in the eggplant and chickpeas.

Heat a large, heavy-based frying pan over medium–high heat, add 3–4 tablespoons of oil and single tablespoon amounts of batter to the pan. Cook for 2–3 minutes on each side or until golden and firm in the centre. Drain on kitchen paper and keep warm. Repeat with the remaining batter.

MAKES 20

1 eggplant (aubergine)

sea salt and freshly ground black pepper

olive oil, for cooking

225 g (8 oz/1½ cups) self-raising (self-rising) flour

250 ml (9 fl oz/1 cup) milk

2 eggs

200 g (7 oz) canned chickpeas (garbanzo), drained, rinsed and roughly mashed

parmesan wafers with
celeriac remoulade and roast beef

Preheat the oven to 180°C (350°F/Gas 4). Line 2 baking trays with baking paper. Place 1-tablespoon amounts of parmesan on the trays, leaving 5 cm (2 inches) between each to allow for spreading. Bake for 8–10 minutes or until golden. Leave to cool on the trays.

Peel the celeriac and coarsely grate into a bowl. Add the mustard, lemon juice and enough cream to bring the mixture together. Season with salt and pepper.

To serve, top each wafer with a spoonful of the remoulade, half a slice of roast beef and garnish with the chives.

MAKES 16

250 g (9 oz/2½ cups) shredded parmesan cheese

1 celeriac (celery root)

2 teaspoons Dijon mustard

2 tablespoons lemon juice

3–5 tablespoons pouring (single) cream

sea salt and freshly ground black pepper

8 slices rare roast beef, halved

snipped chives, for garnish

lentil balls with lime
and smoked paprika

Heat the olive oil in a saucepan over medium heat, add the onion and carrot and sauté for 3–4 minutes or until softened or translucent. Stir in the paprika and harissa and cook for 30 seconds. Add the lentils and stir well. Pour in enough stock to cover, bring to the boil, reduce the heat and simmer, adding more stock as necessary, for 15 minutes or until the lentils are tender and all the liquid has been absorbed. Transfer to a bowl and leave to cool slightly.

Add the coriander, lime zest and egg to the lentil mixture along with enough breadcrumbs to bring the mix just together but is not too dry. Season with salt and pepper. Roll the mixture into golf-ball-sized balls.

Heat the vegetable oil in a deep-fryer or large, heavy-based saucepan to 180°C (350°F) and deep-fry 6–8 balls at a time for 3–4 minutes or until golden. Drain on kitchen paper. Sprinkle with salt and serve.

MAKES 30

2 tablespoons olive oil

1 onion, finely diced

1 carrot, finely diced

1 teaspoon smoked sweet paprika

1 teaspoon harissa

180 g (1 cup) red lentils, rinsed

500 ml (18 fl oz/2 cups) vegetable stock

½ cup chopped coriander (cilantro)

finely grated zest of 2 limes

1 egg

50–100 g (1¾–3½ oz/½–1 cup) dried breadcrumbs

sea salt and freshly ground black pepper

vegetable oil, for deep-frying

wild mushroom tartlets

Pour 250 ml (9 fl oz/1 cup) boiling water over the porcini mushrooms and leave for 20 minutes. Drain, reserving the porcini and soaking liquid.

Heat the oil in a saucepan over medium–high heat, add the onion and cook for 3–4 minutes or until softened and translucent. Add the wild mushrooms and cook, stirring often, for 4–5 minutes or until softened. Add the garlic and porcini and cook for 1–2 minutes or until fragrant. Add the wine and cook until reduced by half. Add the reserved liquid and bring to the boil. Reduce the heat and simmer for 10–15 minutes or until all the liquid has evaporated. Add the chopped parsley and season with salt and pepper.

Spoon the hot mushroom mixture into the tartlet shells. Garnish with the parsley leaves.

MAKES 30–35

10 g (⅓ oz) dried porcini mushrooms

2 tablespoons olive oil

1 onion, finely diced

250 g (9 oz) wild mushrooms, sliced

2 garlic cloves, crushed

80 ml (2½ fl oz/⅓ cup) white wine

2 tablespoons chopped flat-leaf (Italian) parsley or basil

sea salt and freshly ground black pepper

35 savoury tart shells

fresh flat-leaf (Italian) parsley leaves, for garnish

goat's cheese roulade
on bruschetta

Preheat the oven to 180°C (350°F/Gas 4). Place the capsicum on a baking tray and roast for 20 minutes or until the skin has blackened. Transfer to a bowl, cover with plastic wrap and leave for 10 minutes. Remove the skin and seeds. Cut into 4 strips lengthways and set aside.

Meanwhile, lightly brush both sides of the baguette slices with 1½ tablespoons of the olive oil. Place on baking trays and bake for 10 minutes or until lightly golden, turning once. Set aside.

Preheat a barbecue or char-grill pan to medium–high. Brush both sides of the eggplant slices with the remaining olive oil and cook for 2 minutes on each side or until softened and charred. Leave to cool.

Place a large piece of aluminium foil on a surface. Arrange the eggplant, slightly overlapping so there are no gaps, in a 20 cm x 26 cm (8 inch x 10½ inch) rectangle.

Place the goat's cheese and cream cheese in a bowl and beat together until smooth. Spread over the eggplant, scatter over the basil and arrange the capsicum along the centre lengthways. Using the foil as a guide, carefully roll up along the longest side, enclosing the filling, and twist the ends to secure tightly. Refrigerate for 2 hours.

To serve, cut the roulade into thin slices using a sharp knife. Place a slice on a toasted baguette slice, drizzle with the extra-virgin olive oil and garnish with basil leaves.

MAKES 24

1 red capsicum (pepper)

80 ml (2½ fl oz/⅓ cup) olive oil

1 baguette, cut into 1.5 cm (⅝ inch) thick slices

450 g (1 lb) eggplant, cut into 5 mm (¼ inch) thick slices

100 g (3½ oz) goat's cheese

100 g (3½ oz) cream cheese

½ cup basil leaves

extra-virgin olive oil, for drizzling

fresh basil leaves, for garnish

lamb filo rolls
with cinnamon and currants

Preheat the oven to 180°C (350°F/Gas 4). Line 2 baking trays with baking paper.

Heat the oil in a saucepan over medium–high heat, add the shallots and garlic and sauté for 2–3 minutes or until softened and translucent. Add the ginger, cinnamon, cloves and lamb and cook, breaking up any lumps with a wooden spoon, for 5 minutes or until browned. Add the tomato, tomato paste and stock, then cover and simmer for 10 minutes. Remove the lid and cook for a further 10 minutes or until the liquid has almost evaporated. Stir through the currants and almonds and season with salt and pepper.

Lay a sheet of filo on a surface with the short end closest to you, brush generously with the butter and top with another sheet of filo. Repeat once more. Keep the rest of the filo covered with a damp kitchen towel to prevent it from drying out. Cut the buttered filo lengthways into thirds. Place 1 tablespoon of mixture on each of the short ends, fold in the sides to encase the filling and roll each up into a cigar. Seal the ends, place on the trays and brush the tops with butter. Repeat with the remaining filo and mixture. Bake for 15–25 minutes or until golden.

To serve, sprinkle with the cinnamon.

MAKES ABOUT 30

2 tablespoons olive oil

3 French shallots,
 finely chopped

3 garlic cloves, crushed

½ teaspoon ground ginger

1 teaspoon ground cinnamon

¼ teaspoon ground cloves

400 g (14 oz) minced lamb

250 g (9 oz/1 cup) canned
 diced tomato

1 tablespoon tomato paste
 (concentrated purée)

250 ml (9 fl oz/1 cup)
 chicken stock

50 g (1¾ oz/⅓ cup) currants

2 tablespoons chopped almonds

sea salt and freshly ground
 black pepper

375 g (13 oz) filo pastry

melted butter, for brushing

ground cinnamon to serve

baby caramelised onion
tartes tatin

Place the oil, onion and thyme in a frying pan over low heat and cook, stirring regularly, for 20–30 minutes or until softened and caramelised. Season with salt and pepper.

Preheat the oven to 180°C (350°F/Gas 4). Lightly grease two 12-hole mini-muffin trays.

Meanwhile, to make the dough, sift the flour and salt into a bowl and make a well in the centre. Whisk the milk, butter, mustard and egg together in a separate bowl. Add to the dry ingredients and mix with a fork until the dough just comes together. Knead briefly on a floured surface until smooth. Roll out to 1 cm (½ inch) thick and, using a 2.5 cm (1 inch) round cutter, cut into 20 circles.

Place a spoonful of onion in the base of each mini-muffin hole, sprinkle with some cheese and top with a circle of dough. Bake for 10–15 minutes or until golden. Leave in tins for 3–4 minutes. To remove the tartes, cover each tray with a large plate and invert the tartes onto the plate.

MAKES 20

80 ml (2½ fl oz/⅓ cup) olive oil

3 onions, thinly sliced

2 sprigs thyme

sea salt and freshly ground black pepper

50 g (1¾ oz/½ cup) grated cheddar cheese

DOUGH

250 g (9 oz/1⅔ cups) self-raising (self-rising) flour

1 teaspoon salt

100 ml (3½ fl oz) milk

40 g (1½ oz) butter, melted

1 teaspoon Dijon mustard

1 egg

ocean trout tartare
with potato rösti

Peel and finely grate the potatoes. Wrap in a kitchen towel and wring out to remove excess moisture. Transfer to a small bowl, combine with the spring onion and season with salt and pepper. Roll about 2 tablespoons of mixture into tight balls, then flatten into patties.

Heat 5 mm (1/4 inch) oil in a large, heavy-based frying pan over medium heat, add the rösti, in batches, and cook until golden on both sides. Remove, drain on kitchen paper and keep warm.

Finely dice the ocean trout, combine with the lime juice and season.

To serve, spread a little wasabi over each rösti, top with 1 heaped teaspoon of trout tartare and garnish with the pickled ginger and chives.

MAKES 20

500 g (1 lb 2 oz) potatoes

4 spring onions (scallions), thinly sliced

sea salt and freshly ground black pepper

vegetable oil, for shallow-frying

250 g (9 oz) piece of skinless ocean trout fillet, pin-boned

2 tablespoons lime juice

wasabi paste, for spreading

2 tablespoons pickled ginger, finely diced

snipped chives, for garnish

prawn and ginger
money bags

Combine the prawn, garlic, spring onion, ginger, coriander and soy sauce in a bowl.

Lay 6–8 gyoza wrappers on a surface. Keep the rest of the wrappers covered with a damp kitchen towel to prevent them from drying out. Place 1 teaspoon of prawn mixture in the centre of each wrapper. Brush the edge with water, fold up the sides around the filling to form a pouch, pinch at the top to enclose and tie up with a chive to secure. Repeat with the remaining wrappers and mixture.

Heat the oil in a deep-fryer or large, heavy-based saucepan to 180°C (350°F) and deep-fry the money bags, in batches, turning occasionally, for 3–4 minutes or until golden and cooked through. Drain on kitchen paper and keep warm. Serve with the sweet chilli sauce.

MAKES 30

200 g (7 oz) minced prawn (shrimp)

1 garlic clove, crushed

4 spring onions (scallions), thinly sliced

2 teaspoons grated ginger

1 tablespoon chopped coriander (cilantro)

1 tablespoon soy sauce

1 x 250 g (9 oz) packet gyoza wrappers

fresh chives, to tie around money bags

vegetable oil, for deep-frying

sweet chilli sauce, for dipping

gyoza with pork
and kaffir lime

Combine the pork, cabbage, spring onion, sesame oil, soy sauce, ginger, garlic and lime leaves in a bowl.

Lay 6–8 wrappers on a surface. Keep the rest of the wrappers covered with a damp kitchen towel to prevent them from drying out. Place 1 teaspoon of pork mixture in the centre of each wrapper. Brush the edge with water, fold in half, pressing the edge together to seal. Repeat with the remaining wrappers and mixture.

Heat a large, heavy-based frying pan over medium–high heat, add 2 tablespoons oil and 10–12 dumplings but do not overcrowd. Cook for 2–3 minutes or until crisp on one side, then add 125 ml (4½ fl oz/ ½ cup) boiling water, cover, reduce the heat and simmer for 5–6 minutes or until gyoza are cooked through. Remove from the heat, add a splash of soy to the pan and serve gyoza with pan juices. Repeat with the remaining gyoza.

MAKES 50

400 g (14 oz) lean minced pork

50 g (1¾ oz/1 cup) finely shredded Chinese cabbage (wombok)

4 spring onions (scallions), sliced

1 teaspoon sesame oil

1 tablespoon soy sauce, plus extra, for drizzling

2 teaspoons grated ginger

2 garlic cloves, crushed

2 kaffir lime leaves, finely chopped

1 x 200 g (7 oz) packet gyoza wrappers

peanut oil, for cooking

spicy onion
and chickpea bhajis

Blanch the onions in a saucepan of boiling water. Drain well, reserving the onion and 250 ml (9 fl oz/1 cup) cooking liquid.

Place the chickpea flour, plain flour, baking powder, cumin, ground coriander and salt in a bowl and make a well in the centre. Add the egg and reserved cooking liquid and whisk together until smooth. Add the onion, chickpeas and chopped coriander and mix well.

Heat 4 cm (1½ inches) oil in a large, heavy-based saucepan or wok over medium–high heat. Add single tablespoon amounts of mixture to the pan and cook until golden on both sides. Drain on kitchen paper and keep warm. Repeat with the remaining mixture.

Serve with yoghurt dipping sauce.

MAKES 50

3 onions, finely diced

150 g (5½ oz/1 cup) chickpea (besan) flour

150 g (5½ oz/1 cup) plain (all-purpose) flour

2 teaspoons baking powder

3 teaspoons ground cumin

3 teaspoons ground coriander

1 teaspoon sea salt

1 egg

400 g (14 oz) canned chickpeas (garbanzo), drained, rinsed and roughly mashed

⅓ cup chopped coriander (cilantro)

vegetable oil, for shallow-frying

yoghurt dipping sauce, to serve

peking duck
and macadamia wontons

To make the dipping sauce, combine the ingredients in a small bowl and set aside.

Finely dice the duck meat and combine with the ginger, spring onion, coriander, macadamia nuts, hoisin sauce and soy sauce.

Lay 6–8 wonton wrappers on a surface. Keep the rest of the wrappers covered with a damp kitchen towel to prevent them from drying out. Place 1 teaspoon of duck mixture in the centre of each wrapper. Brush 2 edges with water, fold each wonton in half and press edges together firmly to seal. Repeat with remaining wrappers and mixture.

Bring a saucepan of water to the boil. Add wontons, in batches of 6–8, and poach for 3–4 minutes or until the wrapper is translucent.

Serve with the dipping sauce.

MAKES 25

200 g (7 oz) pre-cooked duck breast, skin discarded

2 tablespoons grated ginger

2 spring onions (scallions), chopped

2 tablespoons chopped coriander (cilantro)

40 g (1½ oz/¼ cup) macadamia nuts, chopped

1 tablespoon hoisin sauce

2 teaspoons soy sauce

1 x 250 g (9 oz) packet wonton wrappers

CHILLI-SOY DIPPING SAUCE

80 ml (2½ fl oz/⅓ cup) soy sauce

2 small red chillies, chopped

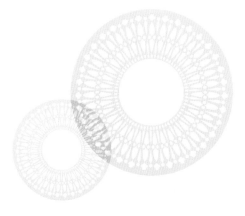

zucchini flower fritters
stuffed with feta and basil

Sift the flour and ½ teaspoon salt together in a bowl and make a well in the centre. Whisk the egg yolk, olive oil and 250 ml (9 fl oz/1 cup) water together in a bowl. Add to the flour and whisk until combined. Leave to rest for 30 minutes.

Meanwhile, gently open each zucchini flower and remove the stamen. Wash gently, if needed, and dry well. Roughly mash the feta using a fork. Add the basil and season with pepper. Place 1 heaped teaspoon of filling into each flower and firmly press the petals around the filling to enclose.

Heat 5 cm (2 inches) vegetable oil in a large, heavy-based saucepan or wok over medium–high heat.

Beat the eggwhite until soft peaks form, then fold through the batter. Dip the zucchini flowers, one at a time, into the batter, then add to the hot oil and cook for 4–5 minutes or until golden. Drain on kitchen paper and season with salt.

MAKES 16

150 g (5½ oz/1 cup) plain
(all-purpose) flour

sea salt and freshly ground black pepper

1 egg, separated

1 teaspoon olive oil

16 zucchini flowers (squash blossoms)

150 g (5½ oz) soft (Persian) feta

10 basil leaves, chopped

vegetable oil, for shallow-frying

prosciutto, roquefort
and rocket arancini

Heat a heavy-based frying pan over medium–high heat, add the prosciutto and cook for 2–3 minutes on each side or until crisp. Chop and set aside.

Heat a large, heavy-based saucepan over medium heat, add the olive oil, onion, garlic, leek, if using, and carrot, if using, and sauté for 3–4 minutes or until softened and the onion and leek are translucent. Add the rice, stir to coat in the oil and cook for 1 minute. Add the wine and stir until absorbed.

Add enough stock to just cover the rice and stir until absorbed. Continue adding stock, a ladleful at a time as each addition is absorbed, and stirring well after each ladleful. After 15–20 minutes the rice should be nearly cooked; each grain should still be slightly firm in the centre. Remove from the heat. Add the prosciutto, cheeses, rocket and parsley and stir until the cheese has melted and the risotto is creamy. Season with pepper.

When the risotto is cool enough to handle, roll the mixture into golf-ball-sized rounds. Lightly whisk the egg and milk together. Place the breadcrumbs in a shallow bowl. Working with one ball at a time, dip each ball in the eggwash, then coat in the breadcrumbs.

Heat the vegetable oil in a deep-fryer or large, heavy-based saucepan to 180°C (350°F) and deep-fry 6–8 balls at a time for 3–4 minutes or until golden. Drain on kitchen paper. Sprinkle with salt to serve.

MAKES 30

6 slices prosciutto

2 tablespoons olive oil

1 onion, finely diced

1 garlic clove, crushed

1 leek, white part only, thinly sliced (optional)

1 carrot, finely diced (optional)

200 g (7 oz/1 cup) arborio rice

125 ml (4½ fl oz/½ cup) white wine

750 ml–1 litre (26–36 fl oz/ 3–4 cups) hot vegetable or chicken stock

50 g (1¾ oz/½ cup) grated parmesan cheese

100 g (3½ oz) Roquefort or other blue cheese

50 g (1¾ oz) rocket (arugula) leaves, chopped

2 tablespoons chopped flat-leaf (Italian) parsley

sea salt and freshly ground black pepper

1 egg

125 ml (4½ fl oz/½ cup) milk

120 g (4¼ oz/2 cups) panko (Japanese) breadcrumbs

vegetable oil, for deep-frying

thai corn fritters

Combine the flour, polenta, baking powder and salt in a bowl and make a well in the centre. Add the egg and milk and mix until smooth. Add the corn, chopped coriander, spring onion and chilli and stir well. If the mixture seems too thin, add 1–2 tablespoons extra flour; if it is too thick, add 1–2 tablespoons extra milk.

Heat a large, heavy-based frying pan over medium heat, add 1–2 tablespoons oil and single tablespoon amounts of mixture and cook for 2–3 minutes or until crisp and bubbles form on the top, then flip over and cook the other side until golden. Remove from the pan and keep warm. Repeat with the remaining mixture. Garnish with the coriander leaves and serve with the sweet chilli sauce.

MAKES 30

150 g (5½ oz/1 cup) self-raising (self-rising) flour, plus 1–2 tablespoons extra

180 g (6½ oz/1¼ cups) polenta

½ teaspoon baking powder

½ teaspoon salt

1 egg

250 ml (9 fl oz/1 cup) milk, plus 1–2 tablespoons extra

400 g (14 oz/2 cups) canned corn kernels, drained

½ cup chopped coriander (cilantro)

4 spring onions (scallions), thinly sliced

1 small red chilli, seeds removed and diced

vegetable oil, for shallow-frying

fresh coriander leaves, for garnish

sweet chilli sauce, for dipping

betel leaves with crab,
kaffir lime and chilli

Combine all of the ingredients, except the betel leaves and salmon caviar in a large bowl. Lay the betel leaves flat on a surface. Divide the mixture between the leaves and top with a few pearls of salmon caviar, if using.

NOTE: Betel leaves are available from Thai grocers.

MAKES 20

150 g (5½ oz) cooked crabmeat

1 long red chilli, seeds removed and sliced

2 kaffir lime leaves, thinly sliced

1 cup coriander (cilantro) leaves

1 red (Asian) shallot, diced

4 mint leaves, thinly sliced

1 tablespoon fried shallots

1 tablespoon lime juice

1 tablespoon fish sauce

20 betel leaves (see note)

50 g (1¾ oz) salmon caviar (roe) (optional)

crisp pork belly
with chilli caramel

Preheat the oven to 170°C (325°F/Gas 3).

Place the lemongrass, garlic, shallot, ginger, chilli and lime zest in a food processor. Reserve a few coriander leaves for garnish and add the remaining leaves, stems and roots to the food processor. Process until a coarse paste forms.

Heat 2 tablespoons of oil in a large, heavy-based, ovenproof saucepan over medium–high heat, add the paste and sauté for 2 minutes or until fragrant. Add the soy sauce, fish sauce, palm sugar and 375 ml (13 fl oz/1½ cups) water and bring to the boil. Add the pork, cover and bake for 1½ hours or until the pork is tender when pierced with a knife. Leave to cool for 4–5 hours.

To make the chilli caramel, place the sugar and 250 ml (9 fl oz/1 cup) water in a saucepan over medium–low heat. Gently bring to the boil, reduce the heat and simmer for 15 minutes or until light golden. Do not stir but occasionally brush down the sides of the pan with water to prevent the sugar from crystallising. Remove from the heat and add 2 tablespoons of water; be very careful as the caramel may spit. Stir in the fish sauce, soy sauce, chilli and star anise. Leave for 1 hour to infuse.

Heat the oil in a deep-fryer or large, heavy-based saucepan to 180°C (350°F). Cut the pork into 2 cm (¾ inch) cubes, dust in the flour and deep-fry for 3–4 minutes or until golden. Drain on kitchen paper.

To serve, divide the pork into small bowls, drizzle over the chilli caramel and garnish with the reserved coriander leaves.

SERVES 6

1 stalk lemongrass, bruised and chopped

4 garlic cloves, chopped

4 red (Asian) shallots, chopped

40 g (1½ oz) ginger, chopped

2 long red chillies, chopped,

finely grated zest of 1 lime

1 bunch coriander (cilantro), plus roots, chopped

vegetable oil, for cooking

125 ml (4½ fl oz/½ cup) soy sauce

2 tablespoons fish sauce

2 tablespoons grated palm sugar

1 kg (2 lb 4 oz) piece of pork belly, rind removed

tapioca flour, rice flour or cornflour, for dusting

CHILLI CARAMEL

250 g (9 oz) caster (superfine) sugar

200 ml (7 fl oz) fish sauce

3 tablespoons light soy sauce

2 small red chillies, finely chopped

3 star anise

rabbit calzones
with porcini and pine nuts

Preheat the oven to 180°C (350°F/Gas 4).

Drain the mushrooms, reserving the liquid, and finely dice. Heat 2 tablespoons of oil in a large, heavy-based, ovenproof saucepan over medium–high heat. Add the rabbit and brown all over. Remove from the pan and set aside. Add the remaining oil, shallot, garlic and thyme to the pan and sauté for 2–3 minutes or until softened and translucent. Add the carrot and cook for 2 minutes. Add the mushrooms, reserved liquid, wine and stock. Bring to the boil, cover, transfer to the oven and bake for 1½ hours or until the meat is falling off the bones.

Meanwhile, make the dough (see page 63 for method).

Remove the rabbit from the pan and shred the meat from the bones. Place the pan back over medium–low heat, add the tomato paste and cook for 10–15 minutes or until the sauce has thickened. Add the rabbit and pine nuts and stir through. Cool.

Preheat the oven to 220°C (425°F/Gas 7). Lightly oil 2 baking trays. Knock back the dough and divide into 20 pieces. Roll each into a ball, place on a floured surface, cover with a kitchen towel and leave for 20–30 minutes or until doubled in size. Flatten each ball into an 8 cm (3¼ inch) round. Place 1 tablespoon of filling onto one half of each round and sprinkle with parmesan. Fold in half and twist the edges together to seal. Place on the trays, brush with oil and bake for 10–15 minutes or until golden.

MAKES 20

15 g (½ oz) dried porcini mushrooms, soaked in 125 ml (4½ fl oz/½ cup) hot water for 20 minutes

3 tablespoons olive oil

600 g (1 lb 5 oz/about ½) farmed rabbit, cut into pieces

3 French shallots, finely diced

2 garlic cloves, crushed

4 sprigs thyme

1 small carrot, finely diced

125 ml (4½ fl oz/½ cup) white wine

125 ml (4½ fl oz/½ cup) chicken stock

1½ tablespoons tomato paste (concentrated purée)

40 g (1½ oz/¼ cup) pine nuts, toasted and chopped

50 g (1¾ oz/½ cup) finely grated parmesan cheese

CALZONE DOUGH

400 g (14 oz/2⅔ cups) plain (all-purpose) flour, sifted

1 x 7 g (¼ oz) sachet dried yeast

2 tablespoons olive oil, plus extra, for brushing

1 tablespoon honey

pinch of salt

wasabi tuna
with cucumber salad

To make the spice mix, heat a frying pan over medium–high heat. Add the cumin and coriander seeds and toast until fragrant and the seeds start to pop. Leave to cool. Place the almonds in a spice grinder and grind to form fine crumbs. Transfer to a bowl. Place the cumin and coriander seeds in the spice grinder and coarsely grind. Add to the ground almond with the wasabi powder and mix well. Place on a plate and set aside.

Soak the wakame in a bowl of water for 5 minutes or until softened. Drain well. Roughly chop and combine with the cucumber, pickled ginger and sesame seeds.

Cut the tuna into 10 cm (4 inch) long pieces and coat well in the spice mix.

Heat the oil in a heavy-based frying pan over high heat, add the tuna and cook for 1 minute on each side or until seared and still pink in the middle; be careful not to overcook. Transfer to a chopping board and, using a sharp knife, cut each piece into 5 x 2 cm (¾ inch) thick pieces.

To serve, place a piece of tuna in a small bowl, top with 1 heaped teaspoon of cucumber salad and drizzle with a little soy sauce.

NOTE: Dried wakame, a type of seaweed, is available from Asian grocers.

MAKES 25–30

1 tablespoon dried wakame (see note)

1 Lebanese (short) cucumber, seeds removed and thinly sliced

2 tablespoons pickled ginger, thinly sliced

1 tablespoon black sesame seeds

1 x 450–500 g (1 lb–1 lb 2 oz) piece of yellowfin tuna

3 tablespoons vegetable oil

soy sauce, for drizzling

SPICE MIX

1 tablespoon cumin seeds

2 tablespoons coriander seeds

1 tablespoon almonds

2 tablespoons wasabi powder

pork and chilli jam tostadas

Preheat the oven to 160°C (315°F/Gas 2–3).

Place the tomato, chilli, adobo sauce, coriander and capsicum in a food processor and process until finely chopped. Set aside.

Heat the oil in a large, heavy-based, ovenproof saucepan over medium–high heat, add the onion and garlic and sauté for 2–3 minutes or until translucent. Add the tomato mixture, wine and stock and bring to the boil. Add the pork, cover, transfer to the oven and bake for 2½–3 hours or until the meat is falling off the bone. Remove the pork from the pan and when cool enough to handle, finely shred the meat from the bones. Season with salt and pepper and set aside.

Meanwhile, to make the chilli jam, place the tomato, chilli, capsicum, onion, garlic and oil in a saucepan over medium–low heat and cook for 1 hour. Add the sugar, increase the heat to medium and cook for a further hour or until the oil starts to separate from the jam. Pour into a sterilised jar and leave to cool.

Increase the oven to 200°C (400°F/Gas 6). Using a 5 cm (2 inch) round cutter, cut 25 rounds from the slices of sourdough. Lightly brush with oil, place on baking trays and bake for 10–15 minutes or until toasted.

To serve, top each toasted round with 1 tablespoon of pork mixture, 1 teaspoon of chilli jam and garnish with a coriander leaf.

NOTE: Chipotle chillies in adobo sauce are available from Latin-American grocers and gourmet food stores. The chilli jam makes about 1½ cups and will keep refrigerated for 2–3 weeks.

MAKES 25

450 g (1 lb/about 6 small) tomatoes, blanched, peeled and chopped

1 chipotle chilli in adobo sauce, plus 1 tablespoon of sauce (see note)

½ bunch coriander (cilantro), plus roots, roughly chopped

1 red capsicum (pepper), roasted and peeled

2 tablespoons olive oil, plus extra, for brushing

1 red onion, finely diced

4 garlic cloves, crushed

125 ml (4½ fl oz/½ cup) white wine

250 ml (9 fl oz/1 cup) chicken stock

500 g (1 lb 2 oz) piece of pork shoulder, bone in

sea salt and freshly ground black pepper

1 loaf rye sourdough, cut into 2 cm (¾ inch) thick slices

CHILLI JAM

450 g (1 lb/about 6 small) tomatoes, blanched, peeled and finely diced

130 g (4⅔ oz/about 5) long red chillies, seeds removed and finely diced

1 red capsicum (pepper), roasted, peeled and finely diced

1 onion, finely diced

4 garlic cloves, crushed

125 ml (4½ fl oz/½ cup) olive oil

110 g (3¾ oz/½ cup) caster (superfine) sugar

coriander (cilantro) leaves, for garnish

manchego croquettes
with sweet capsicum relish

Heat the olive oil in a frying pan over medium–high heat, add the shallot and garlic and sauté until softened and translucent. Stir in the paprika and set aside.

Melt the butter in a saucepan over medium heat, add the flour and cook for 2–3 minutes. Add the milk, a little at a time, stirring well after each addition to prevent lumps forming. Continue stirring for 5 minutes or until the sauce is thick and smooth. Add the shallot mixture and cheese and stir until melted. Season with salt and pepper. Spread onto a tray and refrigerate for 3–4 hours or until set.

Meanwhile, to make the relish, place the tomato, capsicum and onion in a large bowl, sprinkle with the salt and leave for 3–4 hours. Rinse off the salt and drain well. Place in a saucepan with the vinegar, sugar, paprika and cumin over medium heat. Bring to the boil, reduce the heat and simmer for 20–30 minutes or until thickened. Serve at room temperature.

Remove the croquette mixture from the refrigerator and roll single tablespoon amounts into balls. Dip each ball in the egg and roll in the breadcrumbs.

Heat the vegetable oil in a deep-fryer or large, heavy-based saucepan until 180°C (350°F) and deep-fry the croquettes, in batches, for 3–4 minutes or until golden all over. Drain on kitchen paper.

To serve, place 2–3 croquettes in small newspaper cones or bamboo boats with the relish on the side.

NOTE: Manchego, a hard Spanish cheese made from sheep's milk, is available from delicatessens.

MAKES ABOUT 40

3 tablespoons olive oil

4–6 French shallots, finely diced

2 garlic cloves, crushed

2 teaspoons smoked sweet paprika

100 g (3½ oz) butter

125 g (4½ oz) plain (all-purpose) flour

700 ml (24 fl oz) warm milk

100 g (3½ oz) Manchego cheese, finely grated (see note)

sea salt and freshly ground black pepper

2 eggs, lightly beaten

120 g (4¼ oz/2 cups) panko (Japanese) breadcrumbs

vegetable oil, for deep-frying

SWEET CAPSICUM RELISH

250 g (9 oz/about 3) tomatoes, blanched, peeled and finely diced

2 red capsicums (peppers), finely diced

2 onions, finely diced

3 tablespoons salt

250 ml (9 fl oz/1 cup) white vinegar

165 g (5¾ oz/¾ cup) caster (superfine) sugar

½ teaspoon smoked sweet paprika

1 teaspoon ground cumin

pizzettes with goat's milk
camembert and pickled walnut

To make the dough, place all of the ingredients and 250 ml (9 fl oz/ 1 cup) warm water in the bowl of an electric mixer fitted with a dough hook, combine well, then knead on a floured surface for 10 minutes or until smooth and elastic. Place in an oiled bowl, cover with a kitchen towel and leave in a warm place for 1 hour or until doubled in size.

Preheat the oven to 220°C (425°F/Gas 7). Lightly oil 2 baking trays. Knock back the dough and divide into 24 pieces. Roll each into a ball, place on a floured surface, cover with a kitchen towel and leave for 20–30 minutes or until doubled in size. Press each ball into a 7 cm (2¾ inch) round and place onto the trays. Divide the camembert among the rounds, top with 3 slices of tomato and drizzle with a little walnut oil. Bake for 10–15 minutes or until golden.

To serve, top each pizzette with a slice of pickled walnut and some parsley.

NOTE: Walnut oil and pickled walnuts are available from gourmet food stores. Walnut oil is very strongly flavoured, so only use a little.

MAKES 24

250 g (9 oz) goat's milk camembert cheese, thinly sliced

24 cherry tomatoes, sliced into 4

walnut oil, for drizzling (see note)

8–10 pickled walnuts, sliced (see note)

¼ cup flat-leaf (Italian) parsley, finely shredded

PIZZA DOUGH

400 g (14 oz/2⅔ cups) plain (all-purpose) flour, sifted

1 x 7 g (¼ oz) sachet dried yeast

2 tablespoons olive oil

1 tablespoon honey

pinch of salt

fish and fennel pies
with sourdough crust

To make the pastry, place the flour, butter and salt in a food processor and pulse until the mixture resembles breadcrumbs. Add the egg yolks and 80 ml (2½ fl oz/⅓ cup) cold water and pulse again until just starting to come together. Knead on a floured surface to bring together, shape into a disc, wrap in plastic wrap and refrigerate for 1 hour.

Meanwhile, heat the butter in a large, heavy-based saucepan over medium–high heat, add the onion and fennel and sauté for 2–3 minutes or until softened and translucent. Add the flour and mix well. Add 125 ml (4½ fl oz/½ cup) of stock and stir well, ensuring there are no lumps. Gradually add the remaining stock, stirring well. Add the fish, reduce the heat and simmer for 10 minutes, stirring gently until the sauce has thickened. Stir through the cream and parsley, and season with salt and pepper. Leave to cool.

Process the bread in a food processor until roughly chopped. Transfer to a bowl and stir through the parmesan and dill.

Preheat the oven to 190°C (375°F/Gas 5). Lightly grease twenty 6 cm x 2.5 cm (2½ inch x 1 inch) pie tins. Roll out the pastry to 5 mm (¼ inch) thick and, using an 8 cm (3¼ inch) round cutter, cut out 20 circles. Press each circle into the tins, trimming excess pastry. Divide the fish mixture between the tins, top with the breadcrumb mixture and bake for 20–25 minutes or until the tops are golden. Leave to cool slightly, then remove from the tins using a butter knife.

Serve with the mayonnaise and lemon wedges.

MAKES 20

50 g (1¾ oz) butter

1 small onion, finely diced

1 baby fennel, thinly sliced

40 g (1½ oz) plain (all-purpose) flour

375 ml (13 fl oz/1½ cups) hot fish stock

350 g (12 oz) skinless firm white fish fillets, cut into small cubes

3 tablespoons pouring (single) cream

¼ cup chopped flat-leaf (Italian) parsley

sea salt and freshly ground black pepper

2–3 slices day-old sourdough, crusts removed

25 g (1 oz/¼ cup) finely grated parmesan cheese

¼ cup dill leaves

mayonnaise, to serve

lemon wedges, to serve

SHORTCRUST PASTRY

300 g (10½ oz/2 cups) plain (all-purpose) flour

120 g (4¼ oz) cold unsalted butter, cubed

pinch of salt

2 egg yolks

cannellini bean
and chorizo empanadas

To make the dough, combine the milk, yeast and sugar in a bowl and leave in a warm place for 10–15 minutes or until frothy. Place the flour and polenta in the bowl of an electric mixer fitted with a dough hook and make a well in the centre. Lightly beat the eggs and sour cream together, then stir in the yeast mixture. Add to the flour mixture with the butter and mix well to form a dough. Knead on a floured surface for 10 minutes or until smooth and elastic. Place in an oiled bowl, cover with a kitchen towel and leave in a warm place for 1½ hours or until doubled in size.

Meanwhile, heat the oil in a saucepan over medium heat, add the onion and sauté for 1–2 minutes or until translucent. Stir through the spices. Add the chorizo and cook for 1 minute. Add the tomato, stock and beans, bring to the boil, reduce the heat, cover and simmer for 10 minutes. Remove from the heat and mash roughly with a fork. Season with salt and pepper and stir through the coriander.

Preheat the oven to 180°C (350°F/Gas 4). Line 2 baking trays with baking paper. Roll out the dough to 5 mm (¼ inch) thick and, using a 7 cm (2¾ inch) round cutter, cut out 30 circles. Do not re-roll the scraps. Place 1 tablespoon of filling onto one half of each circle, brush the edges with water, fold in half and press to seal. Place on the trays, spray with oil and bake for 15 minutes or until light golden.

Combine the crème fraîche and lime juice and serve with the empanadas.

MAKES 30

1 tablespoon olive oil

½ onion, finely diced

1 teaspoon smoked sweet paprika

1 teaspoon ground cumin

135 g (4¾ oz) chorizo sausage, finely diced

2 small tomatoes, finely diced

125 ml (4½ fl oz/½ cup) chicken stock

400 g (14 oz) canned cannellini beans, drained

sea salt and freshly ground black pepper

¼ cup chopped coriander (cilantro)

250 g (9 oz/1 cup) crème fraîche

juice of 1 lime

EMPANADA DOUGH

125 ml (4½ fl oz/½ cup) warm milk

1 x 7 g (¼ oz) sachet dried yeast

1½ tablespoons caster (superfine) sugar

335 g (11¾ oz/2¼ cups) plain (all-purpose) flour, sifted

225 g (8 oz/1½ cups) polenta

2 eggs

90 g (3¼ oz/⅓ cup) sour cream

80 g (2¾ oz) butter, melted

olive oil spray, for greasing

char-grilled scallops
wrapped in prosciutto

Whisk the oil, lemon juice, garlic, chilli, lemon zest and rosemary together in a bowl. Season with salt and pepper. Add the scallops and toss to coat well.

Wrap a piece of prosciutto around each scallop and secure with a toothpick.

Preheat a barbecue or char-grill pan to medium–high. Cook the scallops for 1–2 minutes on each side or until just cooked.

Serve on a bed of shredded lettuce.

MAKES 24

3 tablespoons olive oil

1 tablespoon lemon juice

2 garlic cloves, crushed

1 small red chilli, finely diced

1 teaspoon finely grated lemon zest

1 teaspoon chopped rosemary

sea salt and freshly ground black pepper

24 scallops, roe removed

12 thin slices prosciutto, halved lengthways

shredded lettuce, to serve

zucchini and haloumi fritters
with roasted capsicum salsa

Preheat the oven to 180°C (350°F/Gas 4). Place the capsicum on a baking tray and roast for 20 minutes or until the skin has blackened. Transfer to a bowl, cover with plastic wrap and leave for 10 minutes. Remove the skin and seeds. Cut the capsicum into thin strips and place in a bowl with the parsley and lemon juice. Set aside until required.

Coarsely grate the zucchini. Wrap in a kitchen towel and wring out to remove excess moisture. Place in a bowl, add the haloumi, spring onion, flour, egg and dill, season with salt and pepper and stir to combine.

Heat 2 cm (¾ inch) oil in a large, heavy-based frying pan over medium heat, add 1 tablespoon of the zucchini mixture, flatten out slightly and cook for 1–2 minutes on each side or until golden. Drain on kitchen paper and keep warm. Repeat with the remaining mixture.

To serve, top each fritter with a spoonful of capsicum salsa.

MAKES 24

1 small red capsicum (pepper)

1 tablespoon chopped flat-leaf (Italian) parsley

1 tablespoon lemon juice

350 g (12 oz/about 3) zucchini (courgettes)

250 g (9 oz/2½ cups) grated haloumi cheese

3 spring onions (scallions), chopped

75 g (2¾ oz/½ cup) plain (all-purpose) flour

2 eggs, lightly beaten

1 tablespoon chopped dill

sea salt and freshly ground black pepper

olive oil, for shallow-frying

crab cakes
with wasabi avocado

Combine the crabmeat, spring onion, garlic, soy sauce, coriander, eggwhite and breadcrumbs in a bowl and season with salt and pepper. Shape 1-tablespoon amounts of mixture into patties.

Heat 2 cm (¾ inch) oil in a large, heavy-based frying pan over medium heat. Cook the patties, in batches, for 1–2 minutes on each side or until golden. Drain on kitchen paper and keep warm. Repeat with the remaining patties.

Mash the avocado, wasabi and lemon juice together in a small bowl and season.

To serve, top each crab cake with some avocado mixture and sprinkle with black sesame seeds and spring onion.

MAKES 24

500 g (1 lb 2 oz) cooked crabmeat

3 spring onions (scallions), chopped, plus extra, for garnish

1 garlic clove, crushed

3 teaspoons soy sauce

1½ tablespoons chopped coriander (cilantro)

1 eggwhite

100 g (3½ oz/1¼ cups) fresh breadcrumbs, made from day-old bread

sea salt and freshly ground black pepper

vegetable oil, for shallow-frying

1 avocado

1 teaspoon wasabi paste

1 teaspoon lemon juice

1 teaspoon black sesame seeds

sri lankan goat curry
golden turnovers

To make the curry powder, heat a frying pan over medium heat, add the rice and toast until lightly browned. Transfer to a bowl. Toast the remaining spices, in batches, until browned and fragrant and add to the rice. Cool, then place in a spice grinder and grind to a powder.

Preheat the oven to 180°C (350°F/Gas 4). Heat 2 tablespoons of the oil in a large, heavy-based, ovenproof saucepan over medium–high heat. Add the goat and brown all over. Remove from the pan. Add the remaining oil, onion, garlic and ginger and sauté for 2–3 minutes or until softened and translucent. Add the curry leaves, turmeric, cinnamon, lemongrass and 3 tablespoons of curry powder and cook for 1 minute or until fragrant. Stir in the tomato, tomato paste and 375 ml (13 fl oz/ 1½ cups) water. Add the goat and juices to the pan, bring to the boil, cover, transfer to the oven and bake for 1½ hours or until tender. Break up the meat and season with salt and pepper. Cool.

Increase the oven to 220°C (425°F/Gas 7). Line 2 baking trays with baking paper. Using an 8 cm (3¼ inch) round cutter, cut out 40 circles from the pastry. Place 1 teaspoon of goat mixture onto one half of each circle. Brush the edges with water, fold in half and press to seal. Place on the trays, brush with the egg and bake for 15 minutes or until golden.

NOTE: Fresh curry leaves are available from Indian and Asian grocers. The curry powder will keep for 2–3 months in a sealed container.

MAKES 40

3 tablespoons olive oil

500 g (1 lb 2 oz) piece of goat shoulder, cut into large pieces

1½ small onions, finely diced

2 garlic cloves, crushed

30 g (1 oz) ginger, finely chopped

1 sprig curry leaves, leaves removed (see note)

¼ teaspoon ground turmeric

2 cinnamon sticks

1 stalk lemongrass, cut into 4 cm (1½ inch) lengths and bruised

4 small tomatoes, finely diced

1 tablespoon tomato paste (concentrated purée)

sea salt and freshly ground black pepper

1.5 kg (3 lb 5 oz) good-quality pre-rolled butter puff pastry, covered with a kitchen towel to prevent drying out

2 eggs, lightly beaten

CURRY POWDER

1 tablespoon long-grain rice

1 cinnamon stick

3 tablespoons coriander seeds

3 tablespoons fennel seeds

1 tablespoon cumin seeds

½ teaspoon cardamom seeds

½ teaspoon black peppercorns

5 cloves

8–10 fresh curry leaves (see note)

2 dried red chillies

north african tuna
and preserved lemon parcels

Combine the tuna, onion, dill, parsley, preserved lemon, cayenne pepper and lime juice in a bowl.

Lay a spring roll wrapper on a surface. Keep the rest of the wrappers covered with a damp kitchen towel to prevent them from drying out. Place 1 tablespoon of mixture in the centre of the wrapper. Make a well in the centre of the mixture, then break a quail egg into the well. Brush the edges of the wrapper with the egg yolk, fold the edge closest to you up over the mix, then fold the opposite edge over the top. Brush the 2 sides with egg yolk, then fold both sides into the middle to form a well-sealed square. Repeat with the remaining wrappers and mixture.

Heat the oil in a deep-fryer or large, heavy-based saucepan over medium heat until 180°C (350°F). Deep-fry the parcels, in batches, for 3–4 minutes or until golden. Drain on kitchen paper.

MAKES 24

1 x 375 g (13 oz) can tuna in olive oil, drained

1 small red onion, finely diced

¼ cup finely chopped dill

¼ cup finely chopped flat-leaf (Italian) parsley

½ preserved lemon, flesh discarded and rind finely chopped

½ teaspoon cayenne pepper

juice of 1 lime

24 small spring roll wrappers

24 quail eggs

3 egg yolks, lightly beaten

vegetable oil, for deep-frying

smoked trout, lime
and quail egg tartlets

To make the pastry, place the flour, butter and salt in a food processor and pulse until the mixture resembles breadcrumbs. Add the egg yolks and 80 ml (2½ fl oz/⅓ cup) cold water and pulse again until just starting to come together. Knead on a floured surface to bring together, shape into a disc, wrap in plastic wrap and refrigerate for 1 hour.

Preheat the oven to 180°C (350°F/Gas 4). Lightly grease twenty-four 6 cm x 1 cm (2½ inch x ½ inch) fluted or plain tartlet tins.

Roll out the pastry to 5 mm (¼ inch) thick and, using an 8 cm (3¼ inch) round cutter, cut out 24 circles. Press each circle into the tins, trimming excess pastry. Place on baking trays and refrigerate for 30 minutes. To blind bake the cases, line them with baking paper and fill with dried beans, rice or baking weights. Bake for 15–20 minutes, remove the beans and paper and bake for a further 10–15 minutes or until golden and cooked through. Leave to cool in tins, then turn out.

Bring a large saucepan of water to the boil. Using a spoon, carefully place the quail eggs into the pan. Bring back to the boil and cook for 1½ minutes. Drain and refresh in cold water. When cool enough to handle, peel and halve lengthways.

Combine the crème fraîche, lime juice and zest in a bowl. Gently fold in the trout. Divide the mixture between the cases, top each with a quail-egg half, garnish with chervil leaf and sprinkle with the black salt.

NOTE: Cyprus black sea salt is available from gourmet food stores.

MAKES 24

12 quail eggs

2 tablespoons crème fraîche

2 tablespoons lime juice

finely grated zest of 1 lime

250 g (9 oz) smoked trout, flaked, skin and bones discarded

fresh chervil, to garnish

Cyprus black sea salt (see note)

SHORTCRUST PASTRY

300 g (10½ oz/2 cups) plain (all-purpose) flour

120 g (4¼ oz) cold unsalted butter, cubed

pinch of salt

2 egg yolks

chicken pizzettes with
rosella paste and macadamia nuts

Make the dough (see page 63 for method).

Meanwhile, to make the paste, remove the rosella seeds from the flowers. Roughly chop the flowers, place in a saucepan and set aside. Place the seeds in a separate saucepan, cover with water and bring to the boil, reduce the heat and simmer for 30 minutes. Strain the liquid, discarding the seeds, and add the liquid to the flowers. Add the apple, cover with water and simmer for 20 minutes. Add the sugar and cook for 20 minutes or until the paste is thick. Pour into a sterilised jar and leave to cool.

Preheat the oven to 190°C (375°F/Gas 5). Season the chicken with salt and pepper. Heat the oil in an ovenproof frying pan over medium–high heat, add the chicken and cook for 1 minute on each side or until browned, then roast for 10–15 minutes or until cooked through. Cool, then cut into small dice.

Increase the oven to 220°C (425°F/Gas 7). Lightly oil 2 baking trays. Knock back the dough and divide into 24 pieces. Roll each into a ball, place on a floured surface, cover with a kitchen towel and leave for 20–30 minutes or until doubled in size. Press each ball into a 7 cm (2¾ inch) round and place onto the trays. Spread each with 1 teaspoon of goat's curd, leaving a 1 cm (½ inch) border and bake for 10–15 minutes or until the bases are crisp and golden. Top each with some chicken and 1 teaspoon of rosella paste, sprinkle with the nuts and garnish with the herbs.

NOTE: Rosella flowers are available from health food stores and gourmet food stores. The rosella paste makes about 500 ml (18 fl oz/ 2 cups). This can be made the day before and will keep refrigerated for 6 months.

MAKES 24

1 x 180 g (6½ oz) skinless chicken breast fillet

sea salt and freshly ground black pepper

2 tablespoons olive oil

200 g (7 oz) goat's curd

35 g (1¼ oz/¼ cup) chopped toasted macadamia nuts

fresh micro herbs, for garnish

PIZZA DOUGH

400 g (14 oz/2⅔ cups) plain (all-purpose) flour, sifted

1 x 7 g (¼ oz) sachet dried yeast

2 tablespoons olive oil

1 tablespoon honey

pinch of salt

ROSELLA PASTE

500 g (1 lb 2 oz) frozen rosella flowers with seeds (see note)

1 small apple, peeled, cored and chopped

330 g (11¾ oz/1½ cups) caster (superfine) sugar

smoked ham and cheddar
quichettes with green tomato pickle

To make the pastry, place the flour, butter and salt in a food processor and pulse until the mixture resembles breadcrumbs. Add the egg yolk and 2 tablespoons cold water and pulse again until just starting to come together. Knead on a floured surface to bring together, shape into a disc, wrap in plastic wrap and refrigerate for 1 hour.

Meanwhile, to make the pickle, place the tomato and onion in a large bowl, sprinkle with the salt and leave for 3–4 hours. Rinse off the salt and drain well. Place in a saucepan with the remaining ingredients. Bring to the boil over medium heat, reduce the heat and simmer for 30–40 minutes or until thickened. Pour into a sterilised jar and leave to cool.

Preheat the oven to 180°C (350°F/Gas 4). Lightly grease twenty-four 6 cm x 2 cm (2½ inch x ¾ inch) fluted or plain tartlet tins. Roll out the pastry to 5 mm (¼ inch) thick and, using an 8 cm (3¼ inch) round cutter, cut out 24 circles. Press each circle into the tins, trimming excess pastry. Place on baking trays and refrigerate for 30 minutes. To blind bake the cases, line them with baking paper and fill with dried beans, rice or baking weights. Bake for 15–20 minutes, remove the beans and paper and bake for a further 10–15 minutes or until golden and cooked through. Remove and set aside to cool in tins.

Divide the ham and cheese between the cases. Whisk together the eggs and cream in a jug and pour into the cases. Bake for 15–20 minutes or until golden and set. Cool slightly and remove from the tins.

To serve, top each quiche with 1 teaspoon of pickle and garnish with thyme leaves.

NOTE: The green tomato pickle makes 2 cups and will keep refrigerated for 4–6 weeks.

MAKES 24

250–300 g (9–10½ oz) double-smoked ham, finely diced

200 g (7 oz) cheddar cheese, finely grated

2 large eggs

3 tablespoons pouring (single) cream

fresh thyme leaves, to garnish

GREEN TOMATO PICKLE

500 g (1 lb 2 oz) green tomatoes, finely diced

2 small onions, finely diced

3 tablespoons salt

1 teaspoon yellow mustard seeds

¼ teaspoon ground turmeric

1 cinnamon stick

6 cloves

200 ml (7 fl oz) white vinegar

150 g (5½ oz) caster (superfine) sugar

SHORTCRUST PASTRY

300 g (10½ oz/2 cups) plain (all-purpose) flour

180 g (6½ oz) cold unsalted butter, cubed

pinch of salt

1 egg yolk

pandan chicken
and black bean parcels

Combine the salted black beans, chilli bean paste and kecap manis in a shallow bowl. Cut each thigh fillet into 4 evenly sized pieces. Add to the salted black bean mixture and coat well. Refrigerate for 1 hour to marinate.

Preheat the oven to 180°C (350°F/Gas 4).

Lay the pandan leaves on a surface. Place 1 piece of chicken at the end of each leaf and roll up into a triangle to enclose. Secure with a toothpick and place on a baking tray. Bake for 10–15 minutes or until cooked through, turning once.

NOTE: Salted black beans, chilli bean paste and pandan leaves are available from Chinese or Thai grocers.

MAKES 20

1 tablespoon salted black beans, soaked in water, drained and finely chopped (see note)

1 tablespoon chilli bean paste (see note)

1 tablespoon kecap manis

500 g (1 lb 2 oz/about 5) skinless chicken thigh fillets

20 pandan leaves (see note)

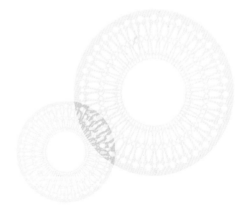

tostadas with chipotle
chicken and guacamole

Bring a saucepan of water to the boil, reduce the heat to medium–low, add the chicken and poach gently for 15 minutes or until cooked through. Drain and, when cool enough to handle, finely shred.

Heat the olive oil in a saucepan over medium heat, add the onion and sauté for 2–3 minutes or until softened and translucent. Add the chilli, tomato, stock, tomato paste and chicken. Bring to the boil, reduce the heat, cover and simmer for 10 minutes. Remove the lid and cook for 10–15 minutes or until the sauce has thickened. Stir through the coriander, lime zest and juice. Season with salt and pepper and keep warm.

Combine the avocado and lemon juice in a bowl and mash together with a fork. Set aside.

Using a 5 cm (2 inch) round cutter, cut out 20 rounds from the tortillas. Heat the vegetable oil in a deep-fryer or large, heavy-based saucepan to 180°C (350°F) and deep-fry the tortilla rounds, in batches, for 2 minutes or until crisp. Drain on kitchen paper.

To serve, top each tortilla round with a smear of mashed avocado and 1 tablespoon of chicken mixture and garnish with a coriander leaf.

NOTE: Chipotle chillies in adobo sauce are available from Latin-American grocers and gourmet food stores.

MAKES 20

1 x 180 g (6½ oz) skinless chicken breast fillet

2 tablespoons olive oil

1 small onion, thinly sliced

1 chipotle chilli in adobo sauce, seeds removed (see note)

250 g (9 oz/1 cup) canned diced tomatoes

250 ml (9 fl oz/1 cup) chicken stock

1 tablespoon tomato paste (concentrated purée)

1 cup chopped coriander (cilantro), plus leaves, for garnish

finely grated zest and juice of 1 lime

sea salt and freshly ground black pepper

1 ripe avocado

2–3 tablespoons lemon juice

5–6 large round corn tortillas

vegetable oil, for deep-frying

fig galettes with jamón
and pepperberry mayonnaise

To make the pastry, place the flour, butter and salt in a food processor and pulse until the mixture resembles breadcrumbs. Add the yolks and 80 ml (2½ fl oz/⅓ cup) cold water and pulse again until just starting to come together. Knead on a floured surface to bring together, shape into a disc, wrap in plastic wrap and refrigerate for 1 hour.

Meanwhile, to make the mayonnaise, whisk the egg, egg yolk and mustard together in a large bowl. While whisking, add the oil in a thin continuous stream until it is all added and the mayonnaise is thick. Whisk in the lemon juice, pepperberry and season with salt. Cover closely with plastic wrap and refrigerate until required.

Preheat the oven to 190°C (375°F/Gas 5). Line 2 baking trays with baking paper. Roll out the pastry to 5 mm (¼ inch) thick and, using a 10 cm (4 inch) round cutter, cut out 24 circles. Place a fig half, cut-side up, on each circle. Bring the pastry up around the fig to encase and pleat the edges to secure. Place on the trays and drizzle with the oil. Bake for 15–20 minutes or until golden.

To serve, top each galette with a slice of jamón, a dollop of mayonnaise and garnish with the parsley leaves.

NOTE: Ground pepperberry is available from specialty Indigenous food suppliers. The mayonnaise makes 1½ cups and will keep refrigerated for 2–3 days.

MAKES 24

12 small figs, halved

olive oil, for drizzling

12 thin slices (about 120 g/ 4¼ oz) jamón Ibérico, halved crossways

flat-leaf (Italian) parsley leaves, for garnish

SHORTCRUST PASTRY

300 g (10½ oz/2 cups) plain (all-purpose) flour

120 g (4¼ oz) cold unsalted butter, cubed

pinch of salt

2 egg yolks

PEPPERBERRY MAYONNAISE

1 egg

1 egg yolk

2 teaspoons Dijon mustard

300 ml (10½ fl oz) vegetable oil

2 tablespoons lemon juice

1 tablespoon ground pepperberry (see note)

sea salt

mini duck pies
with broad bean mash

Preheat the oven to 170°C (325°F/Gas 3). Heat the oil in a large, heavy-based, ovenproof saucepan over medium–high heat, add the duck and brown on each side. Remove from the pan. Add the shallot and garlic to the pan and sauté for 1–2 minutes or until softened and translucent. Add the bacon and cook for 2 minutes. Add the carrot, celery and herbs and cook for 4–5 minutes or until softened. Stir in the wine, stock and jelly. Bring to the boil, arrange the duck on top, cover, transfer to the oven and bake for 1½ hours or until the meat is falling off the bones.

Meanwhile, make the pastry (see page 66 for method).

Remove the duck from the sauce. Place the sauce over medium–high heat and cook for 10 minutes or until thickened. Remove the thyme sprigs. Discard the skin from the duck and shred the meat from the bones. Stir the duck meat back into the sauce and season with salt and pepper. Cool.

Place the potato in a saucepan of water, bring to the boil and cook for 10 minutes or until tender. Drain, add the butter and mash until smooth. Add the broad beans and roughly mash then season.

Increase the oven to 190°C (375°F/Gas 5). Lightly grease twenty 6 cm x 2.5 cm (2½ inch x 1 inch) pie tins. Roll out the pastry to 5 mm (¼ inch) thick and, using an 8 cm (3¼ inch) cutter, cut out 20 circles. Press each circle into the tins, trimming excess pastry. Divide the duck mixture between the tins, top with the mash and bake for 20–25 minutes or until the pastry is golden and crisp. Cool slightly in the tins, then remove using a butter knife.

MAKES 20

2 tablespoons olive oil

3 duck marylands, trimmed

2 French shallots, finely chopped

2 garlic cloves, crushed

50 g (1¾ oz) bacon, finely diced

1 small carrot, finely diced

1 stick celery, finely diced

3–4 sprigs thyme

2 fresh bay leaves

185 ml (6 fl oz/¾ cup) red wine

375 ml (13 fl oz/1½ cups) beef stock

80 g (2¾ oz/¼ cup) redcurrant jelly

sea salt and freshly ground black pepper

2 potatoes, roughly chopped

30 g (1 oz) butter

300 g (10½ oz/3 cups) blanched and peeled broad beans

SHORTCRUST PASTRY

300 g (10½ oz/2 cups) plain (all-purpose) flour

120 g (4¼ oz) cold unsalted butter, cubed

pinch of salt

2 egg yolks

caramelised leek
and artichoke scones

Preheat the oven to 220°C (425°F/Gas 7). Line a baking tray with baking paper.

Heat the butter in a frying pan over medium heat, add the leek and cook for 5 minutes or until softened and golden. Add the sugar and cook for 1 minute. Stir through the artichoke and leave to cool.

Place the flour, baking powder, salt and cubed butter in a food processor and pulse until the mixture resembles breadcrumbs. Add the buttermilk and 150 ml (5 fl oz) cold water and pulse again until the mixture just starts to come together. Tip onto a floured surface, add the leek mixture and bring together quickly with your hands, making sure to not overwork the dough. Pat the dough out to 2 cm (¾ inch) thick. Using a 4 cm (1½ inch) round cutter, cut out 12 rounds and arrange so they are touching on the tray to make a neat 3 x 4 rectangle. Bake for 15 minutes or until light golden.

MAKES 12

40 g (1½ oz) butter

½ leek, white part only, finely diced

1 tablespoon soft brown sugar

2 marinated artichoke hearts, roughly chopped

500 g (1 lb 2 oz/3⅓ cups) self-raising (self-rising) flour

2 teaspoons baking powder

pinch of salt

100 g (3½ oz) cold unsalted butter, cubed

150 ml (5 fl oz) buttermilk

cauliflower galettes
with taleggio and walnuts

To make the pastry, place the flour, butter and salt in a food processor and pulse until the mixture resembles breadcrumbs. Add the yolks and 80 ml (2½ fl oz/⅓ cup) cold water and pulse again until just starting to come together. Knead on a floured surface to bring together, shape into a disc, wrap in plastic wrap and refrigerate for 1 hour.

Meanwhile, bring a saucepan of water to the boil, add the cauliflower and cook for 3–4 minutes or until tender. Drain and refresh in cold water. Heat the olive oil in a frying pan over medium heat, add the shallot and sauté for 1–2 minutes or until softened and translucent. Add the caraway seeds and cauliflower and cook for 3 minutes. Season with salt and pepper. Leave to cool slightly.

Preheat the oven to 190°C (375°F/Gas 5). Line 2 baking trays with baking paper. Roll out the pastry to 5 mm (¼ inch) thick and, using a 10 cm (4 inch) round cutter, cut out 24 circles. Divide the Taleggio between the circles and top with the cauliflower mixture. Bring the pastry up around the filling to encase and pleat the edges to secure. Place on the trays and bake for 15–20 minutes or until golden.

To serve, drizzle over a little walnut oil and garnish with the walnuts and parsley leaves.

NOTE: Walnut oil is available from gourmet food stores. It is very strongly flavoured so only use a little.

MAKES 24

250 g (9 oz) cauliflower, cut into
  small florets

2 tablespoons olive oil

3 French shallots, finely diced

1 teaspoon caraway seeds

sea salt and freshly ground black pepper

250 g (9 oz) Taleggio cheese,
  thinly sliced

walnut oil, for drizzling (see note)

30 g (1 oz/¼ cup) chopped walnuts

flat-leaf (Italian) parsley leaves,
  to garnish

SHORTCRUST PASTRY

300 g (10½ oz/2 cups) plain
  (all-purpose) flour

120 g (4¼ oz) cold unsalted butter, cubed

pinch of salt

2 egg yolks

crumpets with goat's curd
and lavender honey

Combine the yeast, 1 teaspoon of sugar and 1 tablespoon warm water in a bowl and leave in a warm place for 10–15 minutes or until frothy.

Heat the milk and 80 ml (2½ fl oz/⅓ cup) water in a saucepan over low heat.

Place the flour, salt and bicarbonate of soda in a large bowl and make a well in the centre. Place the egg yolk and remaining sugar in a separate bowl and whisk together until pale and fluffy. Whisk in the yeast mixture and warm milk. Pour into the dry ingredients, stirring well to make sure there are no lumps.

Whisk the eggwhite until stiff peaks form, then gently fold through the batter.

Heat a large non-stick frying pan over medium–high heat. Spray the pan with vegetable oil and add single tablespoon amounts of batter to the pan, cooking 4 crumpets at a time. Cook for 2–3 minutes or until the edges start to dry and holes start to form, then flip over and cook for a further minute. Remove from the pan and keep warm under a kitchen towel. Repeat with the remaining batter.

To serve, top each crumpet with a heaped teaspoon of goat's curd and drizzle with the honey.

NOTE: Lavender honey is available from gourmet food stores.

MAKES ABOUT 24

½ teaspoon dried yeast

3 teaspoons caster (superfine) sugar

125 ml (4½ fl oz/½ cup) milk

150 g (5½ oz/1 cup) plain (all-purpose) flour, sifted

pinch of salt

¼ teaspoon bicarbonate of soda (baking soda), sifted

1 egg, separated

vegetable oil spray

250 g (9 oz) goat's curd

lavender honey (see note)

saffron chicken pies

Heat the oil in a saucepan over medium–low heat, add the shallot, garlic and spices and sauté for 1 minute. Add the chicken and cook for 3 minutes or until browned all over. Add 375 ml (13 fl oz/1½ cups) water, cover, reduce the heat and simmer for 1–1½ hours or until the meat is falling off the bone.

Meanwhile, to make the filling, heat the oil in a frying pan over medium–low heat, add the almonds and cook until golden. Drain on kitchen paper and cool, then process with the sugar in a food processor until fine crumbs form.

Remove the chicken from the pan and, when cool enough to handle, shred the meat from the bones. Combine the meat with the egg and herbs and season with salt and pepper.

Preheat the oven to 190°C (375°F/Gas 5). Line 2 baking trays with baking paper. Lay a sheet of filo on a surface. Keep the rest covered with a damp kitchen towel to prevent it from drying out. Brush half the sheet generously with the butter and fold in half. Brush with more butter and fold in half again. Trim to make a square. Place 1 tablespoon of chicken mixture in the centre and top with 1 teaspoon of filling. Brush the edges with butter and fold one edge up over the mix, then fold the opposite edge over the top. Brush the sides with butter and fold into the middle to form a well-sealed square. Place on a tray. Repeat with the remaining filo, mixture and filling. Bake for 15–20 minutes or until golden.

To serve, dust the pies lightly with icing sugar and cinnamon.

MAKES 20

3 tablespoons olive oil

3 French shallots, roughly chopped

4 garlic cloves, bruised

1 teaspoon saffron threads

¼ teaspoon ground turmeric

1 teaspoon ground ginger

1 teaspoon ground cinnamon, plus extra, for dusting

900 g (2 lb/about 4) skinless chicken thighs, bone in

2 eggs, lightly beaten

¼ cup finely chopped flat-leaf (Italian) parsley

¼ cup finely chopped coriander (cilantro)

sea salt and freshly ground black pepper

20 sheets filo pastry

melted butter, for brushing

icing (confectioners') sugar, for dusting

ALMOND FILLING

3 tablespoons olive oil

80 g (2¾ oz/½ cup) blanched almonds

1 tablespoon caster (superfine) sugar

barramundi burgers
with lemon myrtle mayonnaise

To make the buns, place the flour, yeast, salt and lemon myrtle in the bowl of an electric mixer fitted with a dough hook and make a well in the centre. Add the oil and 170 ml (5½ fl oz/⅔ cup) warm water and mix on low speed to combine. Knead on a floured surface for 15 minutes or until the dough is smooth and elastic. Place in an oiled bowl, cover with a kitchen towel and leave in a warm place for 45 minutes or until doubled in size.

Meanwhile, make the mayonnaise (see page 90 for method, substituting lemon myrtle for pepperberry).

Preheat the oven to 250°C (500°F/Gas 9). Line 2 baking trays with baking paper. Divide the dough into 20 pieces. Roll each into a ball and place on the trays. Press lightly to flatten, sprinkle with salt and lemon myrtle and drizzle with the oil. Leave in a warm place for 30 minutes or until doubled in size. Bake for 15–20 minutes or until golden.

Roughly chop the fish in a food processor. Transfer to a bowl, combine with the lemon zest, season with salt and pepper and shape into 20 patties. Dust each in flour, dip in the egg and press in the breadcrumbs.

Heat the oil in a large frying pan over medium–high heat and cook the patties, in batches, for 2–3 minutes on each side or until cooked through.

To serve, halve each bun, place a patty on the bottom halves, top with a dollop of mayonnaise, sandwich with the tops and secure with a toothpick.

NOTE: Ground lemon myrtle is available from specialty Indigenous food suppliers. The mayonnaise makes 1½ cups and will keep refrigerated for 2–3 days.

MAKES 20

600–650 g (1 lb 5 oz–1 lb 7 oz) skinless barramundi fillets, cut into pieces

finely grated zest of 1 lemon

sea salt and freshly ground black pepper

plain (all-purpose) flour, for dusting

2 eggs, lightly beaten

120 g (4¼ oz/2 cups) panko (Japanese) breadcrumbs

80 ml (2½ fl oz/⅓ cup) olive oil

BURGER BUNS

300 g (10½ oz/2 cups) strong bread flour, sifted

1 tablespoon dried yeast

1 teaspoon salt

1½ teaspoons ground lemon myrtle, plus extra, for sprinkling (see note)

3 tablespoons olive oil

LEMON MYRTLE MAYONNAISE

1 egg

1 egg yolk

2 teaspoons Dijon mustard

300 ml (10½ fl oz) vegetable oil

2 tablespoons lemon juice

½ tablespoon ground lemon myrtle (see note)

beef and sherry pastries

Heat 2 tablespoons of the oil in a large, heavy-based saucepan over medium–high heat, add the beef and brown all over. Remove the beef from the pan. Add the remaining oil, shallot and garlic and sauté for 2–3 minutes or until softened and translucent. Add the carrot, leek and bay leaves and cook for 2 minutes. Return the beef to the pan. Add the tomato, sherry and 60 ml (2¼ fl oz/¼ cup) water, bring to the boil, reduce the heat, cover and simmer for 1½ hours or until the beef is fork-tender.

Meanwhile, to make the pastry, place the flour, butter and salt in a food processor and pulse until the mixture resembles breadcrumbs. Add the egg yolks and 80 ml (2½ fl oz/⅓ cup) cold water and pulse again until just starting to come together. Knead on a floured surface to bring together, shape into a disc, wrap in plastic wrap and refrigerate for 1 hour.

Preheat the oven to 200°C (400°F/Gas 6). Line 2 baking trays with baking paper.

Combine the flour and 2 tablespoons water to make a paste. Add to the beef with the tomato paste. Cook, uncovered, for 10–15 minutes or until the sauce has thickened. Season with salt and pepper and cool.

Roll out the pastry to 5 mm (¼ inch) thick and, using a 10 cm (4 inch) round cutter, cut out 30 circles. Place 1 tablespoon of mixture in the centre of each pastry round. Bring the 2 sides up to meet at the top and pinch together, making a frill. Place on the trays, brush with the egg and bake for 20–25 minutes or until golden.

MAKES 30

3 tablespoons olive oil

350 g (12 oz) stewing beef, cut into 2 cm (¾ inch) dice

2 French shallots, finely diced

2 garlic cloves, crushed

1 small carrot, finely diced

½ leek, white part only, finely diced

2 fresh bay leaves

250 g (9 oz/about 3 small) tomatoes, finely diced

125 ml (4½ fl oz/½ cup) fino (dry) sherry

1 tablespoon plain (all-purpose) flour

1 tablespoon tomato paste (concentrated purée)

sea salt and freshly ground black pepper

1 egg, lightly beaten

SHORTCRUST PASTRY

300 g (10½ oz/2 cups) plain (all-purpose) flour

120 g (4¼ oz) cold unsalted butter, cubed

pinch of salt

2 egg yolks

�֍ index

Published in 2011 by Hardie Grant Books

Hardie Grant Books (Australia)
85 High Street
Prahran, Victoria 3181
www.hardiegrant.com.au

Hardie Grant Books (UK)
Dudley House, North Suite
34–35 Southampton Street
London WC2E 7HF
www.hardiegrant.co.uk

National Library of Australia Cataloguing-in-Publication Data:

Bitesize: tartlets, quichettes & cute things.
ISBN 9781742701172 (pbk.)
Pies – Quiches (Cooking).
641.8652

Designer Trisha Garner
Editor Belinda So
Recipe writers Lee Blaylock, Michele Curtis and Kerrie Sun
Photographer Marina Oliphant
Stylist Caroline Velik
Home economists Andrea Geisler, Peta Gray and Lucinda Macdougall
Props provided by Bison Australia, ferm LIVING, Great Dane Furniture,
Mark Tuckey, Mud Australia, Nord Living and Safari Living
Colour reproduction by Splitting Image Colour Studio
Printed in China by 1010 Printing International Limited